STUDY TO SHOW YOURSELF APPROVED

How to Study the Bible

Dr. Bruce Hitchcock

Study to Show Yourself Approved, © 2018 Dr. Bruce Hitchcock

Published by Books for Ministry a nonprofit 501 (c)(3) Limited Liability Corporation, Escondido, CA. 92026, All Rights Reserved.

Printed in the United States of America

Published by Books for Ministry a 501(c) 3 tax exempt nonprofit corporation. Providing spiritual growth materials to those who can least afford them. For more information, see www.equippingchurches.net.

First Edition: 06/10/2018

ISBN-13: 978-1721081066

ISBN-10: 1721081062

Unless otherwise noted, Scriptures taken from the Holy Bible, New International Version®, NIV®. Copyright © 1973, 1978, 1984, 2011 by Biblica, Inc.™ Used by permission of Zondervan. All rights reserved worldwide. www.zondervan.com The "NIV" and "New International Version" are trademarks registered in the United States Patent and Trademark Office by Biblica, Inc.™

When quoting from this book please cite the following for copyright purposes: Used by permission Bruce Hitchcock, *Study to Show Yourself Approved*, © 2018, published by Book for Ministry, equippingchurches.net, all rights reserved.

(Doctor of Commerce and Ministry, Honoris Causa, California Baptist University, 2017).

Table of Contents

Donor Information 7
Introduction 9
Who do we Focus on in Bible Study? 15
Why Study the Bible? 21
Which Bible do you Choose? 27
How to Study the Bible? 31
What are the Elements of Bible Study: 49
When do We Study the Bible? 61
Where do we Study the Bible? 67
Closing Thoughts 69
Notes 70
Appendix A: Navigator's One Year Bible Reading Plan 71
Appendix B: Recommended commentaries and authors 76

Donor Information

The author's purpose is to produce books and other Christian tools that are biblically accurate, theologically sound, and useful for instruction in spiritual growth (2 Timothy 2:15, 2 Timothy 3:16-17). The salvation of unbelievers, the personal spiritual growth of believers, and the development of those who will disciple others in the future are paramount to the author (Psalms 71:18).

The purchase of this book and the other books and materials by this author are offered directly to consumers for a small donation to "Books for Ministry" a 501 (c) (3) LLC.

"Books for Ministry" donates books to disciplers who then use them to lead others to salvation and disciple believers who cannot afford quality materials. We distribute our books in the United States and where possible, around the world.

For information on "Books for Ministry," to make a donation to receive a book, or to make direct donations, go to our website at equippingchurches.net.

Introduction

Know, Grow, And Show

God wants us to KNOW His Word the Bible.

> Bible study is not the same thing as Bible reading. If Bible reading is like raking for leaves, Bible study is like digging for diamonds. The Christian life calls for both.[1] – John Piper

> *To the Jews who had believed him, Jesus said, "If you hold to my teaching, you are really my disciples. Then you will know the truth, and the truth will set you free" (John 8:31-32).*

God wants us to GROW spiritually: Being Transformed into His Image.

> God gave us the Bible not just to inform our minds, but also to transform our hearts.[2] – John Piper

> *Do not conform to the pattern of this world but be transformed by the renewing of your*

---

[1] John Piper, Basics for How to Study the Bible, © 2018 John Piper, desiringgod.org/basics-for-how-to-study-the-bible.
[2] John Piper, How to Read the bible for Yourself, © 2018 John Piper,

> *mind. Then you will be able to test and approve what God's will is--his good, pleasing and perfect will* (Romans 12:2).

God wants us to SHOW our Lives to Others.

> *In the same way, let your light shine before others, that they may see your good deeds and glorify your Father in heaven* (Matthew 5:16).

> *For we are God's handiwork, created in Christ Jesus to do good works, which God prepared in advance for us to do* (Ephesians 2:10).

Galatians 5:16 tells us that if we walk in the Spirit we will have no desire for the things of the flesh. God's expectation, then, is for us to be living a life that helps us resist temptation. When we are walking in God's light (1 John 1:7) we have fellowship with Jesus and His blood continually cleanses us from our disobedience.

As a testimony to our walking witness of Christ in our lives, Paul says this to the Church at Thessalonica, "*We sent Timothy, who is our brother and co-worker in God's service in spreading the gospel of Christ, to strengthen and encourage you in your faith.*"

What is the Bible

1. <u>The Bible is the Word of God</u>

---

desiringgod.org/articles/how-to-read-the-bible-for-yourself.

We know that it is His Word because God claims that it is His Word. John 1:1 (NIV) makes a true statement that "*In the beginning was the Word, and the Word was with God* (statement A), *and the Word was God.*" Not only is God's Word infinite (Matthew 24:35), it was there before the beginning of all things (John 1:1). God claims that the Word is God Himself (John 1:1b)."

> I wrote for them the many things of my law, but they regarded them as something foreign…First, then, concerning this book: Who is the author? The text says that it is God. "*I have written to him the great things of my law.*" Here lies my Bible—who wrote it? …This Bible is God's Bible, and when I see it, I seem to hear a voice springing up from it, saying, "I am the book of God; man, read me. I am God's writing; open my leaf, for I was penned by God; read it, for he is my author, and you will see him visible and manifest everywhere." "I have written to him the great things of my law."[3]
> – Charles Spurgeon

2. The Bible is Eternal

I am the Alpha and the Omega, the

---

[3] Charles Spurgeon, *The Bible*, Public Domain, A Sermon (No. 15) Delivered on Sabbath Evening, March 18, 1855, by the REV. C. H. Spurgeon At Exeter Hall, Strand, romans45.org/spurgeon/sermons/0015.htm.

Beginning and the End," says the Lord, "who is and who was and who is to come, the Almighty" (Revelation 1:8, NKJV).

God always was, He is right now, and He always will be. Since God is a triune spirit and body, the same eternal nature not only belong to the Father, but also to the Son, and to the Holy Spirit. All three have and will always exist. Since God, in the form of the Trinity, is eternal, with no beginning or ending, His Word(s), the Bible, is also eternal. Simply said, God is eternal (Psalm 102:12), the Word is God (John 1:1), therefore, the Word is eternal.

3. The Bible is inerrant or without error

In 2 Timothy 3:16 the Spirit of God writes this through the apostle Paul, *"All Scripture is God-breathed and is useful for teaching, rebuking, correcting and training in righteousness,"*

> The Bible is inspired but is it inerrant, that is without errors? The reason for a positive answer is simple: The Bible is the Word of God, and God cannot err; therefore, the Bible cannot err. To deny the inerrancy of the Bible one must either affirm that God can err or else that the Bible is not the Word of God.[4] – Norman L. Geisler

The word inerrant means to be without error(s). It

---

[4] Norman L. Geisler, *The Inerrancy of the Bible*, namb.net/apologetics/the-inerrancy-of-the-bible.

is infallible. Since we can see from our previous argument that the Word of God is God's words, and we know that God is without error, therefore, His word is errorless.

4. <u>The Bible is Truth</u>

> The Bible is not only without error it is completely true. *"The entirety of Your word is truth, and every one of Your righteous judgments endures forever"* (Psalm 119:160, NKJV).

> *"Let God be true, and every human being a liar"* (Romans 3:4).

Jesus makes the claim in John 14:6 that He is the truth, *"I am the way and the truth and the life. No one comes to the Father except through me."*

5. <u>The Bible is Complete in Itself</u>

> *The precepts of the LORD are right, rejoicing the heart; The commandment of the LORD is pure, enlightening the eyes. The decrees of the LORD are firm, and all of them are righteous* (Psalm 19:8-9b, NASB)

In Psalm 19:8-9b we see three interesting benefits of the words of God. First, we see that since God's Word is right (righteous), He will give us a rejoicing heart. Secondly, God's message is pure (without any spot). Finally, we see that God's Word is firm (not wavering). Since the Word of God is complete, it will help us to be upright and stable in our ways (Psalm 119:11).

The Bible is designed to meet all our needs and answer all our questions. It is the transformative encyclopedia of God. The Bible explains who God is, why He made us, His plan for us, and describes the future of both the righteous and unrighteous (Psalm 1).

The Word of God is:

1. God's Word: (John 1:1)

2. Eternal: *Your word, LORD, is eternal; it stands firm in the heavens* (Psalm 119:89).

3. Unchanging: *Every good and perfect gift is from above, coming down from the Father of the heavenly lights, who does not change like shifting shadows* (James 1:17).

4. Inerrant: *Sanctify them by the truth; your word is truth* (John 17:17).

5. Our Guide: Your word is a lamp for my feet, a light on my path (Psalm 119:1-5.

6. Pure: *Every word of God is pure: he is a shield unto them that put their trust in him* (Proverbs 30:5).

Who do we Focus on in Bible Study?

Our Focus

The Focus in our study of the Scriptures should always be on God the Father, God the Son, and God the Holy Spirit.

1. <u>God the Father</u>:

God is the planner, creator, and He overseers of all of His creation. The power of God is in all things. That power keeps all creation moving forward according to His plan.

> *Ah, Sovereign Lord, you have made the heavens and the earth by your great power and outstretched arm. Nothing is too hard for you (Jeremiah 32:17).*

2. <u>God the Son</u>:

Jesus is the Son of God. He is the facilitator of God's plan for mankind. It is through the life, suffering on the cross, the death of His body, and the bodily resurrection that we have been justified.

> *For in him all things were created: things in heaven and on earth, visible and invisible, whether thrones or powers or rulers or authorities; all things have been created through him and for him. He is before all things, and in him, all things hold together.*

> *And he is the head of the body, the church; he is the beginning and the firstborn from among the dead, so that in everything he might have the supremacy* (Colossians 1:16-17).

3. God the Spirit:

> *And you also were included in Christ when you heard the message of truth, the gospel of your salvation. When you believed, you were marked in him with a seal, the promised Holy Spirit, who is a deposit guaranteeing our inheritance until the redemption of those who are God's possession--to the praise of his glory* (Ephesians 1:13-14).

The Holy Spirit is the Spirit of God. He is the giver of life and provides for the security of the believer. He is the seal of our salvation (2 Corinthians 1:21-22).

> *The Spirit gives life; the flesh counts for nothing. The words I have spoken to you-- they are full of the Spirit and life.* (John 6:63).

He lives in us to convict us of our disobedience and to teach us about the righteousness of God. He will remind us of all the teachings of Jesus while He was here with us (John 14:26).

> *But very truly I tell you, it is for your good that I am going away. Unless I go away, the Advocate will not come to you; but if I go, I will send him to you. When he*

comes, he will prove the world to be in the wrong about sin and righteousness and judgment: about sin, because people do not believe in me; about righteousness, because I am going to the Father, where you can see me no longer; and about judgment, because the prince of this world now stands condemned (John 16:7-11).

The Holy Spirit is important to the study of the Scriptures for several reasons:

<u>The Spirit gave us the Word</u>:

2 Peter 1:20-21 tells us that *"Above all, you must understand that no prophecy of Scripture came about by the prophet's own interpretation of things. For prophecy never had its origin in the human will, but prophets, though human, spoke from God as they were carried along by the Holy Spirit."*

The Holy Spirit is the author of the Word of God. The words may have been written on parchment scrolls by men chosen especially by God, but the words that they recorded were given to them by inspiration from His Spirit. These men were God' scribes, writing what the Spirit instructed them to write. 2 Timothy 3:16 supports this understanding when it says, *"All Scripture is breathed out by God and profitable for teaching, for reproof, for correction, and for training in righteousness, that the man of God may be complete, equipped for every good work."*

<u>The Spirit reminds us of the Word</u>:

John 14:26 explains, *"But the Advocate, the Holy Spirit, whom the Father will send in my name, will teach you all things and will remind*

you of everything I have said to you."

The Spirit works in us helping us remember what we have read. When we are in situations that require Scripture, the Holy Spirit reminds us of the verses we have read and learned.

<u>The Spirit interprets Scripture</u>: 1 Corinthians 2:13 says, "*This is what we speak, not in words taught us by human wisdom but in words taught by the Spirit, explaining spiritual realities with Spirit-taught words.*"

The Spirit explains the "*spiritual realities*" that He has taught us from the Word. He clarifies God's words for us so that we can understand how to apply them to our own lives and use them to explain God and His salvation to others.

The Trinity: Working Together

> *I have swept away your offenses like a cloud, your sins like the morning mist. Return to me, for I have redeemed you* (Isaiah 44:22).
>
> *Being justified as a gift by His grace through the redemption which is in Christ Jesus* (Roman 3:24).
>
> *He redeemed us in order that the blessing given to Abraham might come to the Gentiles through Christ Jesus, so that by faith we might receive the promise of the Spirit* (Galatians 3:14).

The single most important action of God's grace is found in redemption. God's complete redemptive plan is revealed within the act of grace (Ephesians 1:7-10). God has explained His plan through His Word the Bible. We read that past grace was declared as mankind was redeemed from the curse of Adam's sin (Romans 5:19). Then, there is the present reality of our own salvation through that redemption as clarified in Colossians 1:13-14. Finally, we envision the future hope of the final act of redemption in the resurrection of the saints in Ephesians 4:30. All three of these expressions of God's grace, past, present and future are a result of the action of Jesus on the cross (Hebrews 9:14-15). We are redeemed by the blood of the Lamb (1 Peter 1:19).

God's grace is displayed in His love. It is impossible for us to fathom the love that God has for His children. It is this love that sent Jesus to the cross to die for our sin. The love that prompted God to expose Jesus to the full force of His wrath. Lastly, the love that persuaded Jesus to willingly accept that pain and suffering for those who have believed in Him and have made Him their Lord (Romans 10:9-10.)

Our Purpose

> *The Lord is not slow in keeping his promise, as some understand slowness. Instead he is patient with you, not wanting anyone to perish, but everyone to come to repentance* (1 Peter 3:9).

God's desire is for the conversation of mankind. Redemption forges transformation. In the production of steel, the steelworkers smelt or heat the iron ore at extremely high temperatures to remove the impurities from the raw ore. They then add carbon to give the purified ore strength and durability. In the redemptive action of Christ, we are the raw material that is transformed by the amazing power of the Holy Spirit.

The transformative power of God removes our impurities. The Spirit of God indwells us, and we are filled with the strength and durability to resist future sin. Just as the brittle, formless, dull iron ore is converted into the purified, shining metal to be used for a purpose, we are changed into the image of God, a new creation, to be used for His purpose.

> *Therefore, if anyone is in Christ, the new creation has come: The old has gone, the new is here* (2 Corinthians 5:17)!

All three members of the Trinity played and continues to play an integral part in these sacrificial actions of grace. It was God who planned redemption before the foundation of the world (Ephesians 1:3-5). The plan was realized through the birth, life, shed blood, resurrection, and ascension of Jesus Christ (vss. 6-9). Finally, the act of redemption finds its fruition in the power and personal presence of the Holy Spirit living and working in and through us (vs. 10 and Hebrews 9:14).

Why Study the Bible?

> The Bible is unique in its production, preservation, proclamations, and product. In its production, it is a harmonious and unified message of redemption that has emerged out of diversity of authors, circumstances, and literary forms. In its preservation, it has miraculously withstood the ravages of time, persecution, and criticism, and continues to be the bestselling book in the world. In its proclamations, it stands alone in its revelation of God's plan from eternity to eternity and in its life-giving message. In its product, it has changed the course of history, reached more people, and transformed more lives than any other book.[5] – Kenneth Boa

God Commands that We Study the Bible

> *Study to show yourself approved unto God, a workman that needs not to be ashamed, rightly dividing the word of truth* (2 Timothy 2:15, NKJV).

Studying the Bible is not a suggestion. God commands us to study His Word. Our goal in the Christian life is transformation. Our salvation (Ephesians 2:8-9) is the

---

[5] Kenneth Boa, *Studying the Scriptures*, © 2018 Bible.org, All Rights Reserved, bible.org/article/studying-scriptures.

first step in a process called sanctification (1 Corinthians 6:11). Sanctification means to be set apart (Hebrews 10:10). We have been set apart for God's use (Ephesians 2:10). At salvation, we become a new creation (2 Corinthians 5:17). However, this is only the beginning of the process of sanctification.

God wants us to experience continual transformation. Romans 12:2 says, *"Do not conform to the pattern of this world but be transformed by the renewing of your mind. Then you will be able to test and approve what God's will is-- his good, pleasing and perfect will."* The command is to be transformed by renewing our minds. This will allow us to learn the will of God for our lives. Understanding the will of God will help us to determine our actions and allow us to fulfill the plan that He has for our lives. The renewing of our minds that accomplishes transformation comes from studying His Word, the Bible.

God Commands Us to Live Obedient Lives.

We discover how to live within God's guidelines by reading, studying, and memorizing His Truth, the Bible. As we read, understand, and apply the Word of God to our lives, in obedience to Him, we are growing in our knowledge, our assurance of Salvation, and eternal life. All this along with establishing a stronger Christian worldview that will impact our daily walk and influence the lives of others.

1 John 1:7 tells us that *"if we walk in the light, as he is in the light, we have fellowship with one another, and the blood of Jesus, his Son, purifies us from all sin."*

John14:5 (ESV) continues, "If you love me, you will keep my commandments."

Acts 5:29 (ESV) says, "But Peter and the apostles answered, "*We must obey God rather than men.*"

1 Peter 1:14 (ESV) explains *"As obedient children do not be conformed to the passions of your former ignorance."*

1 John 5:3 (ESV) teaches, *"For this is the love of God, that we keep his commandments. And his commandments are not burdensome."*

God's Expectation and Priorities for the Believer

<u>Putting God at the Center of Our Lives</u>

To experience God in the center of our lives means to begin by placing Him first in our lives. *"So, whether you eat or drink or whatever you do, do it all for the glory of God"* (1 Corinthians 10:31).

Bible Study is all about Priorities

The things that we feel are most important in our lives are the things we choose. If God is the most important thing in our lives, we will put Him first.

To be in control of time, it helps if Christians prioritize it. Not just prioritizing the activities and events that capture time, but time itself. There are twenty-four hours in a day, which means that there are one-hundred and sixty-eight hours in a week. Sleep takes about fifty-six hours, leaving one-hundred twelve waking hours each week for action.

Believers can and should block out segments of this waking time with strategic activities such as Prayer and Bible study, family time, spiritual community activities, work, recreation, etc. Once the blocks have been identified and prioritized, then the actions and events within each box should be arranged by importance and a maximum amount of time allotted to each one.[6] – Winning at Life

Here is a list of life priorities, from my book "Winning at Life" that honor God and give Him the place He deserves.

God-Centered Life Priorities

We must prioritize our lives in a way that serves and pleases God. The following is a list of the priorities that God establishes for His disciples in the order of their importance to Him.

1. Prayer: alone in your quiet time and with your family (1 Thessalonians 5:17).

2. Bible Study: alone in your quiet time and with your family (2 Timothy 2:15).

3. Family Time: fulfilling the Godly expectations of being a parent (Ephesians 5:30-6:4).

4. Church: "*not giving up meeting together, as some are in the habit of doing, but encouraging one another*" (Hebrews 10:25).

5. Ministry and Evangelism: Community Service and Outreach: (James 1:27).

6. Work: Our work is also an opportunity for spiritual outreach. Everyone has something in their lives that is disconcerting. They desire someone to reach out to them. This makes our ability and desire to pray for others an excellent motivation to ask not just how things are going, but "do you have something in your life that you would like me to pray for?"

---

[6] Bruce Hitchcock, *Winning at Life*, © 2015 Bruce Hitchcock, All Rights Reserved. Pg. 231.

One Christian praying for another about sin in their lives, it still is applicable to prayer for all people. If we are following God's leading, the prayer of a righteous person is both powerful and effective.

7. <u>Recreation and Relaxation</u>: downtime is critical to rejuvenating our bodies. God's example of a Sabbath is a good one for all mankind (Genesis 2:2).

Spiritual Priorities Delineated

It is not until we develop the spiritual habits necessary for giving God first place in our lives that we can adequately live a life of obedience.

1. <u>Prayer life</u>: Let Chronicles 16:10 be the guide, *"Look to the LORD and his strength; seek his face always."*

2. <u>Scripture reading and memorization</u>: Psalm 119:11 says, *"I have hidden your word in my heart that I might not sin against you."*

3. <u>Understanding of Scripture</u>: Proverbs 2:4-6 explains, *"and if you look for it as for silver and search for it as for hidden treasure, then you will understand the fear of the LORD and find the knowledge of God. For the LORD gives wisdom; from his mouth come knowledge and understanding."*

4. <u>Relationship with God</u>: Revelation 3:20 teaches us about the relationship that comes with salvation, *"Behold, I stand at the door and knock. If anyone hears my voice and opens the door, I will come in to him and eat with him, and he with me."*

5. <u>Relationship with others</u>: Hebrews 10:24 gives us a guideline when it says, *"And let us consider how we may spur one another on toward love and good deeds,"*

6. <u>Evangelism</u>: Matthew 28:19 commands that we,

"Therefore go and make disciples of all nations, baptizing them in the name of the Father and of the Son and of the Holy Spirit."

7. <u>Discipleship</u>: Matthew 28:20 continues the commandment when it says, *"teaching them to obey everything I have commanded you. And surely, I am with you always, to the very end of the age."*

8. <u>Worship attendance</u>: Psalm 122:1 expresses the joy that comes from our regular attendance at worship, *"I was glad when they said unto me, Let us go into the house of the LORD.."*

9. <u>Giving</u>:1 Corinthians 4:2 explains our responsibility when it says, *"Now it is required that those who have been given a trust must prove faithful."* Malachi 3:10 tells gives us direction and explains the blessing we will receive from God, *"Bring the whole tithe into the storehouse, that there may be food in my house. Test me in this," says the LORD Almighty, "and see if I will not throw open the floodgates of heaven and pour out so much blessing that there will not be room enough to store it."*

10. <u>Living a Lifestyle of Obedience for Others to See</u>: 1 Kings 8:60-61 instructs us, *"so that all the peoples of the earth may know that the LORD is God and that there is no other. And may your hearts be fully committed to the LORD our God, to live by his decrees and obey his commands, as at this time."*

Which Bible do you Choose?

"Major Bible translations typically reflect one of three general philosophies: formal equivalence, functional equivalence, optimal equivalence."[7] Dave Croteau

Different Types of Translations

Formal equivalence is also referred to as a **WORD-FOR-WORD TRANSLATION** and attempts to translate the Bible as literally as possible, keeping the sentence structure and idioms intact if possible (**King James Version, New King James Version, American Standard Bible, and New American Standard Bible**).

Functional equivalence is typically referred to as a **THOUGHT-FOR-THOUGHT** translation. This is an attempt to translate the text, so it has the same effect on the current reader as it had on the ancient reader (*New International Version, New Living Translation or the Amplified Version*).

Optimal equivalence falls between the former approaches by **BALANCING THE TENSION BETWEEN ACCURACY AND EASE OF READING**. While striving for precision in translation, it also seeks clarity to the modern-

---

[7] Dave Croteau, Transitional Philosophy: – Three Views, © 2018 The Gospel Coalition, All rights Reserved, thegospelcoalition.org/article/translation-philosophy-three-views/.

day reader (*English Standard Version, The Holman Christian Standard Bible, and the Christian Standard Bible*). [8]

Paraphrase: Most paraphrases are written using available Bible texts. However, a few use the original language. Paraphrases attempt to place the Bible in a **CONVERSATIONAL LANGUAGE** that is for the masses (*The Message, The Living Bible, and The Voice*).

Major Study Bibles:

It is helpful if you are going to study the Bible and not just read it, to have a "Study Bible." Study Bibles are different from regular Bibles in that they have interpretative and/or historical notes from an outside authority or authorities.

1. Understand the Faith Study Bible – Zondervan.

With a host of international contributors and editors—including Christianity Today's very own editor-in-chief, Mark Galli—the NIV Understand the Faith Study Bible gives readers answers and insights regarding questions about Christian doctrine, thinkers, and more.

2. NLT Christian Basics Bible – Tyndale

Whether you're a new Christian or simply wanting to go "back to the basics" of Scripture, this Bible is for you. With accessible notes, cross-references, maps, infographics, and more, the NLT Christian Basics

---

[8] Adapted from an article written by Dave Croteau, *Translation Philosophy*, Copyright © 2018 The Gospel Coalition, Inc. All Rights Reserved, thegospelcoalition.org/article/good-and-angry/.

Bible provides a critical starting point—or returning point—for any believer.

3. <u>CSB Apologetics Study Bible</u> – Broadman & Holman

Want to learn how to stand up for your beliefs from Lee Strobel, Chuck Colson, and more? The CSB Apologetics Study Bible provides material from dozens of apologetics thinkers, with study notes, articles, and profiles of Christian historical figures also included.

4. <u>NIV Cultural Backgrounds Study Bible</u> – Zondervan

We all know our English Bibles are translations of writings from thousands of years ago, for audiences in vastly different cultures and contexts from our own. This study Bible offers a glimpse into how real people lived their lives in ancient times, giving a "behind-the-scenes" look at the traditions, historical events, and other influences that shaped the biblical texts.

5. <u>ESV Systematic Theology Study Bible</u> – Crossway

Curious about how certain Christian tenets and beliefs are specifically rooted in particular passages of the Bible? The ESV Systematic Theology Study Bible examines "how Scripture forms the basis for our understanding of God, humanity, sin, salvation, and eternity," with hundreds of notes and articles to help you gain an even deeper understanding of Christian doctrines.

6. <u>NKJV Apply the Word Study Bible</u> – Thomas Nelson

"Practical": that's the best way to describe the NKJV Apply the Word Study Bible. Filled with notes and maps to provide historical context, feature articles, and sidebar material to help readers see "the relevance of

Scripture for everyday living," this Bible is perfect for anyone seeking to ponder God's Word while also directly applying it to their day-to-day life.

7. <u>NIV Faith and Work Bible</u> – Zondervan

What does your faith in God have to do with your job? The answer—whether you're a pastor, a stay-at-home mom, or a 9-5 office employee—is "everything." In this study Bible, each book has an introduction that outlines how it applies to both work and faith, and various stories, articles, and essays are included to inspire and encourage you in your everyday work.[9]

My two personal favorites would be the *CSB Apologetics Study Bible* published by Broadman & Holman (about $30.00 in hardcover) and the *NKJV Apply the Word Study Bible* – Thomas Nelson (approximately $25.00 in hardcover). These two study Bibles have a different focus, and both would be a welcome addition to any Bible Study library.

The addition of a study Bible to a biblical study library does not mean that we do not have an everyday Bible. Most specialty Scriptures are very large and heavy. Even though it is possible to carry the study Bible to church or small group, and individual study sessions, the weight might necessitate the ownership of a lighter standard edition of the Bible.

---

[9] Emily Lund, *Top 7 Study Bibles*, © 2018 Christianity Today - a 501(c)(3) nonprofit organization, christianitytoday.com/biblestudies/articles/bibleinsights/top-7-study-bibles.html.

How to Study the Bible?

While the Bible is an inspired revelation from the living God, it requires our response before it can have an impact upon our lives. Scripture is indeed "profitable for teaching," but its profit does not stop on the level of doctrine; it must move from the head to the heart to accomplish the purpose for which it was given.[10] – Kenneth Boa

Rules for Bible Study

1. Always Begin with Prayer:

We need to recognize who God is as our Lord and Master, praise His holy name, and thank Him continually for what He has done and will continue to do in our lives. In addition to this ongoing recognition of God's greatness and intercession on our behalf, we must ask the Holy Spirit to open our hearts and our minds to understand the written word and its application to our lives. Prayer opens the door to spiritual growth.

2. Find a Quiet Place:

When studying alone, find a quiet place to study away from life's interruptions. Eliminate as much of the noise and other distractions as possible. Turn off the

---

[10] Kenneth Boa, Studying the Scriptures, Ibid.

ringer on your phone. Since Bible study requires focus, quiet is essential.

3. <u>Ask the Right Questions</u>:

<u>Question #1</u>:

After reading a verse or section of Scripture, ask, "What does this verse or Scripture say?" God is speaking to us through His word. The first thought may reveal the truth of that scripture. For instance, John 14:6, says, "Jesus answered, "*I am the way and the truth and the life. No one comes to the Father except through me.*"

At first glance, we may say, "This verse tells us that Jesus provides salvation because He is the way, truth, and the life. He is the only way since no one can come to God except through Him." Now that the interpretation is recorded, it is time to test what has been discovered to see if that is what God wants us to understand about the verse. On the internet, we find an entry that is a sermon by Charles Spurgeon. In this message Spurgeon makes this statement, "But there is no way to heaven, whatever our hopes may be, but through Christ.[11] We see from the Spurgeon explanation that our initial understanding is the correct one.

<u>Question #2</u>:

Ask, who is speaking? John 14:6 says that it is Jesus who is making this claim. Therefore, we know that the statement is truthful, since it is directly from the author of our salvation.

---

[11] Charles Spurgeon, *The Way to God*, Sermon number 245, Public Domain, archive.spurgeon.org/sermons/0245.php

Question #3:

What is the context in which it was said? In our example of John 14, we see that in the first four verses Jesus is explaining that the disciples should not be afraid because He is going to prepare a place for them and that He will come back for them. In verse 5 Thomas says, we don't know where you are going nor, do they know the way.

Then, in 14:6, Jesus tells that that He is the way. In 14:7, Philip says, if you show us the father that will suffice. Jesus, in John 14:9-11, explains that anyone who has seen Him has already seen the Father. He is saying, in a few words, the father and I are one and the same. Therefore, Jesus qualifies to be our redeemer because He is God in Human flesh.

Question #4:

How does this verse apply to my life? If we confess verbally, orally, to God and others, that Jesus is Lord (God), and believe with all our hearts that God raised Him from the dead, we will be saved (Romans 10:9-10). In other words, if we recognize that He is the way, truth, and life (John 14:6) and we confess it, we will receive God's free gift of salvation. We now have the assurance of our salvation through this study (1 Timothy 1:15, Romans 1:16, and Galatians 3:13-15).

4. <u>Always Verify Conclusions</u>:

We must always find other scriptures and outside credible resources that authenticate the results of our study.

5. <u>Scripture Always has the Final Say</u>:

    Every outcome must be substantiated by other scriptures. The following verses affirm John 4:16"

Salvation is to be found through him alone; in all the world there is no one else whom God has given who can save us (Acts 4:12).

If you confess that Jesus is Lord and believe that God raised him from death, you will be saved. For it is by our faith that we are put right with God; it is by our confession that we are saved. (Romans 10:9-10).

Therefore, since we have been justified through faith, we have peace with God through our Lord Jesus Christ (Romans 5:1).

6. <u>Make Bible Study a Habit</u>:

    Schedule Bible study time just like any other activity that is vital to life. Calendar it every day. God is the most important person in our lives. Since He controls all things that happen in our lives, except for sin, we should place Him first in our lives. Bible study allows us to know God better and draw closer to Him. Put Him first every day.

Prayer is Essential to Understanding:

1. <u>Prayer Establishes a Foundation for Interpretation</u>: First Things First

    "May my cry come before you, LORD; give me understanding according to your word" (Psalm 119:169).

    Whether we use deductive (a logical process using multiple premises to establish truth) or inductive reasoning (combining multiple truths to make a conclusion), we must always begin to interpret the meaning of the scripture by praying for direction and understanding from the Holy Spirit.

<u>Consider God</u>: Consider who God is and praise and thank him for His love that has brought us salvation and eternal life. "Thank you, God, for sending Your only son to live and die and rise again. Thank You for the life eternal we have received by believing and accepting that truth."

<u>Clear your mind</u>: Ask God to clear your mind of all the stress, pressure, and unnecessary thoughts that hinder us from focusing on Him and His Word. "Oh Lord, my Lord, give me a clear mind as I go through my day that I may know your will and direction for my life. Help me to transform your word into obedient actions that I might better serve you now and in the future."

<u>Cleanse your heart</u>: Ask God to forgive you for the times you have been disobedient to Him, those you remember and those things you may not remember or be aware of. Pray Psalm 51:10, *"Create in me a pure heart, O God, and renew a steadfast spirit within me."* "Cleanse me this day that I might have a clear connection to You, Oh, Lord."

<u>Celebrate God</u>: Praise God for who He is, what He has done in the past, His current position in our lives, and what He will accomplish through us in the future. Pray Psalm 150:1-2, *"Praise the LORD. Praise God in his sanctuary; praise him in his mighty heavens. Praise him for his acts of power; praise him for his surpassing greatness."* "Praise you, Lord, for you are the only God. You are all knowing, all powerful, and ever-present in and

outside your creation, and in me. Praise your Holy Name forever!"

<u>Convey Thanksgiving to God</u>**:** Approach God with a heart of thanksgiving.

Thank Him for giving us life in Jesus. Thank Him for His provision, guidance, and direction in our lives. "Thank you, Jesus, for all that you have and will do in my life. Help me to honor you in all that I say and all that I do. Forgive me when I err and convict me to repent when I do."

<u>Concede and Consent</u>: 1 Peter 5:6 says, *"Humble yourselves, therefore, under God's mighty hand, that he may lift you up in due time."* We must show our humility to God. He is a loving and forgiving God. We are insignificant. Let Him know that we will follow His direction for our lives as it is revealed in His Word.

Thank Him for graciously listening to us and for all the miracles He has and will continue to do in our lives. "Keep me humble, Oh Jesus, that I might understand my need for You and Your grace and mercy every moment of every day. Help me to know my place and accept it."

2. <u>Sample Prayers from Scripture</u>*:*

> *Search me, O God, and know my heart: try me, and know my thoughts, see if there is any offensive way in me, and lead me in the way everlasting* (Psalm 139:23-24).

> *I pray that the eyes of My heart may be enlightened in order that I may know the hope to which he has called me, the riches of his glorious inheritance in his holy people,*

and his incomparably great power for me who believes. That power is the same as the mighty strength (Ephesians 1:18-19).

Even though I walk through the valley of the shadow of death, I fear no evil, for You are with me; Your rod and Your staff, they comfort me. You prepare a table before me in the presence of my enemies; You have anointed my head with oil; My cup overflows. Surely goodness and lovingkindness will follow me all the days of my life, And I will dwell in the house of the LORD forever (Psalm 23:4-6).

3. Pray Seeking God's Wisdom

Always seek God's wisdom in applying the scripture, when applicable. God has promised us that He will give us wisdom if we ask for it. Matthew 6:33 says this about seeking God, "*But seek first his kingdom and his righteousness, and all these things will be given to you as well.*" James 1:5 tells us that if we lack wisdom ask God, "*If any of you lacks wisdom, you should ask God, who gives generously to all without finding fault, and it will be given to you.*"

4. Pray with Pure Intent

James 15:16b explains that "*The prayer of a righteous person is powerful and effective.*" Righteousness is living according to the faith given to us by the will of God (Romans 1:17). Romans 8:5 makes the concept of the righteous life simple but not easy when it says, "*Those who live according to the flesh have their minds set on what the flesh desires, but those who live in accordance with the Spirit have their minds set on what the Spirit desires."* Walk in the light of His Word (1 John 1:7). Pray with a purity of heart (1 John 1:9).

Choosing a Method, Book, Passage, or Topic:

A helpful hint to understanding and the retention of the thoughts, lessons, and applications of the Scriptures is to read each verse slowly and carefully. Don't be in a rush to cover as much text as possible in the time you have set aside for study. Reading slowly and with understanding helps us to interpret what the passages say. Interpretation is essential to both comprehension and application.

1. Read the Bible Through in One Year:

It has been my experience, after many years of interaction with other believers by teaching a myriad of Bible classes and preaching, that most Christians have never read the entire Bible. It seems a daunting task. The old question is, "How do you eat an Elephant." The answer is, "One bite at a time." The same is true of reading the Scriptures. When we read a small amount of the Bible and do it religiously (no pun intended), it becomes easy. Reading the Bible from cover to cover in one year is an excellent way to get an overview of the entire Word of God.

There are many good sources for reading the Scriptures through in one year. My recommendation would be to use the Navigators website at www.navigators.org. From the home page click on Resources and then from the pulldown choose Bible Study. Then scroll down the page and find Bible Reading Plans. Click on Bible Reading Plans and go to Book at a Time Reading Plan and click on download. You will see a chart that can be downloaded to your computer or printed for your use for free. (See Appendix #1 for the complete reading plan.)

2. <u>Where to Start</u>: Beginning Book Studies: A Good Starting Point:

One of the best methods of studying the Scriptures is the book study. In a book study, we read, study, and apply an entire book of the Bible.

Most new Christians are encouraged to begin in the gospels with the book of John. John's theme and approach is to show the love of God and the love and caring nature of His Son, Jesus. John gives us a great introduction to Jesus and God's plan for redemption and eternal life through Him.

3. <u>Book Studies</u>: Additional Recommendations

Luke: After the reader has completed the Gospel of John, it is recommended that they read the Gospel of Luke. Luke is a more technical book since its author was well educated and a doctor. Luke has written a gospel that is a detailed narrative of the life of Jesus. He says in Luke 1:4, *"so that you may know the certainty of the things you have been taught."* Luke gives us a look at the historical Jesus.

Genesis: Genesis gives us the history of the beginning of all things. This history book discusses the creation of the universe and of mankind (Genesis 1), the first sin (Genesis 2), the first mention of the redemption through the resurrection of Jesus (Genesis 3), the blood sacrifice and the first murder (Genesis 4), the flood and Noah's covenant with God (Genesis 6-10), the great dispersion

(Genesis 11), Abraham and Sarah and an introduction to salvation by faith through Christ alone (Genesis 12-24), the history of Isaac and the rise of Jacob and the birth of the nation Israel (Genesis 25-36), and finally the account of Joseph and the history of God's people in Egypt (Genesis 37-50).

Through the Book of Genesis, we learn about the love that God has for his chosen people portrayed in many different ways and under varied circumstances all out of the sovereign plan and purpose of God to redeem a people who would love and glorify Him for eternity.

Romans: The book of Romans reveals the answers to important questions and supplies information on many topics, such as salvation, the sovereignty of God, judgment, spiritual growth, and the righteousness of God. Many scholars also describe it as The Gospel and the Righteousness of God, which can be received only by faith in the atoning death of Jesus Christ.[12]

Romans is a mini-theology text. In this book, Paul expounds on the great theological terms and concepts that lay the foundation for all we believe.

Psalms: The Psalms include praises of joy, laments, blessings, and thanksgivings. They are directed at God and they help us to express and communicate ourselves to Him. We read about the Psalmist's emotions from one

---

[12] Jay Smith, *The Ultimate Bible Summary Collection*, © Jay Smith Scribd Inc.,
scribd.com/lists/3851369/The-Ultimate-Bible-Summary-Collection-contains-all-66-bible-book-summaries.

extreme to another, from praising, delighting in and worshiping God with fervor, to repentance and crying out to Him in despair.[13]

Proverbs: Proverbs accomplishes something no other biblical book does: it simply compiles numerous short instructions for living an effective life on earth. While other books articulate profound theological truths, lengthy narratives of triumph and failure, or prophetic preaching to a disobedient people, Proverbs concerns itself completely with instructing people in the path of wisdom.[14]

Reading these spiritual primers will lay a solid foundation for all Bible study in the future.

4. The Topical Study: It's Something we Heard or Read

The Topical study is another good way to study the Bible. We hear the pastor, in a study, or in a conversation discussing a particular topic. We can study that topic to become more familiar with what the Bible says about it. Go to the internet and type in the topic and then type in "verses" or "scriptures."

For example, someone in a study might use the term "gospel." For more information on the gospel just type in "gospel verses" and you will see sites that have multiple verses from the Bible with the word gospel in them.

You may want to choose a theme like sin, redemption, forgiveness, love, or wisdom.

---

[13] Jay Smith, ibid.
[14] Chuck Swindoll, *Proverbs*, © 2018 Insight for Living Ministries. All rights

Or you may study a concept like speech, the family, stewardship, or work.[15]

Keep a pen and paper (or computer/iPad) nearby so that notes can be taken from those verses that apply to the topic being examined. These notes will be invaluable as a list of topics and their interpretations for use in future studies.

5. <u>Word Studies</u>: We Have a Question

Many times, we will be reading a verse or section of scripture and discover a word with which we are unfamiliar. Since the word is necessary to our understanding of the verse and the context of the verse or section, we can't ignore it and continue. It's time for a word study. The Holy Spirit will help us, but His expectation is that we do the work. However, He will direct us to the answer. We remember what we discover. Doing the work brings its own reward.

In Bible study, personal discovery, directed by the God's Spirit brings its own reward. Our joy is magnified by the effort. The greatest reward is found in the accomplishment itself. Once we have learned how the word is used and have discovered its context, the Spirit will help us remember, decipher the meaning, apply it to our lives, where practical, and we will find that He gives us opportunities to use the discovery to honor and glorify Him.

When in the process of exploring the meaning and

---

reserved. insight.org/resources/bible/the-wisdom-books/proverbs
[15] Kenneth Boa, Studying the Scriptures, Ibid

context of a word, take notes on the findings. The reasons for studying the Scriptures are multipurpose. There will be many times in the future that the words, their content, substance, and relevance to life in varying degrees and instances, will be essential to forming new attitudes and expressions leading to spiritual growth. Word studies are an extremely important and life-changing method of Bible study.

6. <u>Verse by Verse Studies</u>: Seeking Context

> Interpret every passage in light of its immediate context (preceding and following verses, paragraph, chapter) and broad context (book, testament, Bible). A verse lifted out of its context can become a pretext. It is not as easy to twist the meaning of a verse when it is observed in its setting.[16] – Kenneth Boa

7. <u>Observation</u>: The Reasoning Method

Observation is vital to understanding. Accurate observation means using the first thought that we receive when reading a scripture.

First thoughts give us a theory or premise that becomes a starting point for interpretation. Careful observation combined with accurate investigation promote proper interpretation and life-changing application.

The observation method of Bible study answers the questions who, what, where, when, why and how.

---

[16] Kenneth Boa, Ibid.

After we have finished a section of scripture that seems to begin and end a thought, we ask these six questions to determine as much as possible from our answers.

All investigative thought is based on these six questions and their answers. Observation is a key element in Bible study since it answers views each section of scripture from a variety of views.

8. Correlation

When we consider that there are sixty-six books in the Bible all written about from the same basic theme, the fall of mankind and their journey toward reparation, there is going to be an overlap of thought. In addition to the duplication of thoughts and Scriptural truth, the authors will, from time to time, quote each other to make or highlight a point.

Example #1: Jesus, in the New Testament, Quotes God from the Old Testament.

Many people believe and some even teach that Jesus was condensing the Ten Commandments when in Matthew 22:37, He was asked in verse 36, *"Teacher (Master in a few translations), which is the great commandment in the law?"* In verse 37, "Jesus replied: *"Love the Lord your God with all your heart and with all your soul and with all your mind."* However, He was quoting from Deuteronomy 6:5 which says, *"Love the LORD your God with all your heart and with all your soul and with all your strength."*

By studying both of these scriptures and the correlative verses found in Mark 12:30-31 and Luke 10:27 we will have a deeper understanding of the context and meaning of this important concept. Furthermore, we will grasp that fact that God Himself originally gave us the condensed version to express the importance of loving God completely as our number one goal.

Example #2: Paul, in the New Testament, quotes David in the Old Testament.

In the New Testament, Paul, Romans 3:10, writes, *"As it is written: There is no one righteous, not even one."* In the Old Testament King David writes in Psalms 14:3b, *"there is no one who does good, not even one."*

9. Application

There are two reasons to study God's Word. The first is to understand God and His plan for our lives. The second reason is to apply God's teaching to our lives that we might live in obedience to Him. Application of Scripture is, therefore, vital.

Applying the interpretation to our lives helps us to live in God's will.

I have hidden your word in my heart that I might not sin against you (Psalm 119:11).

God commands us to grow spiritually. We only grow as we apply His word to our lives. When reading passages in Scripture ask these questions:

- a) Are there any promises that I can claim in these verses?
- b) Is there a command that I need to obey?
- c) Are there any sins that I need to avoid?
- d) Is there an example to follow?

e) What encouragement or comfort may I gain?

f) What new perspective is God showing me?[17]

God commands us to walk as children of light by walking in the Spirit. Here are some verses that are examples of the truth of the obedience of the believer.

> "*Like newborn babies, crave pure spiritual milk, so that by it you may grow up in your salvation, now that you have tasted that the Lord is good*" (1 Peter 2:2-3).
>
> "*So I say, walk by the Spirit, and you will not gratify the desires of the flesh. For the flesh desires what is contrary to the Spirit, and the Spirit what is contrary to the flesh. They are in conflict with each other, so that you are not to do whatever you want*" (Galatians 5:16-17).
>
> "*For you were once darkness, but now you are light in the Lord. Live as children of light*" (Ephesians 5:8-10).
>
> "*Anyone who lives on milk, being still an infant, is not acquainted with the teaching about righteousness. But solid food is for the mature, who by constant use have trained themselves to distinguish good from evil*" (Hebrews 5:13-14).

---

[17] by IFL's Pastoral Ministries, How Can I get Started Studying the Bible, Copyright © 2018, Crosswalk.com., All rights reserved., crosswalk.com/devotionals/how-can-i-get-started-studying-the-bible-11633143.html.

Biographical

With the Biographical Method of Bible Study, we select a biblical person and research the Scriptures to study his or her life and character. we try to become thoroughly acquainted with that person's inner life and find out what made it a spiritual success or failure. We ask God to help us think and feel with us so that our study becomes a life-changing experience.

1. Start with a person on whom you can do a simple study.
2. The secret of a good biographical study is to live with that person during the study.
3. Be careful not to confuse different people who have the same name when you look up the references about them.
4. Be careful to find the various names that may apply to just one person.
5. Stay away from books written about biblical people until after you have exhausted every Bible reference about that person and have drawn every possible insight out of those texts.[18]- Rick Warren

In the land of Uz there lived a man whose name was Job. This man was blameless and upright; he feared God and shunned evil. He had seven sons and three daughters, and he owned seven thousand sheep, three thousand camels, five hundred yoke of oxen and five hundred

---

[18] Rick Warren, *Bible Study Methods*, © 1981, 2006, by Rick Warren, published by Zondervan, Grand Rapids, Michigan, 49530, p. 101.

donkeys, and had a large number of servants. He was the greatest man among all the people of the East (Job 1:1-3).

If we were to do a study of Job, a person of great interest in the Old Testament, we would find out almost everything about Him in the book that bears his name, Job. Just these first three verses tell us a great deal about Job. He lived in a land called Uz. Job was blameless, upright, feared God and despised and avoided evil. He was the "greatest man" in the East.

To complete the study, we should read the biographical book (Job) written about him and then ask a few questions. Who is this man Job? What was his greatest personal asset? When did he live? Where is Uz? Why did God choose him to resist the devil? How did Job perform in the light of his trials? What can we learn from this book that will help us to be like Job?

A Point of Interest:

While recording topical studies, questions will arise that cannot be answered at that time. In addition, there will be answers that need a higher level of biblical understanding to interpret. Whenever you are reading the Bible, record these scriptures and those explanations that cannot be explained. These difficult words or phrases of interest that aren't quite clear yet, can be considered later.

What are the Elements of Bible Study:

Interpretation:

Interpretation is the action of Bible study by which we seek to find the meaning of a word, verse, or section of scripture. It is important that we read slowly enough to have a complete understanding of what the text is saying to us. Speeding through the text to reach the goal of finishing a chapter or book may lead to the misinterpretation or inaccurate observation of the content and/or context of individual phrases or whole sections.

The Bible is a whole book. It is not a collection of unrelated stories. It is an account of the fall of mankind and their redemption from that original sin that lead to spiritual death. With this basic understand as a foundation for all scripture, Genesis through Revelation, accurate interpretation of every word in the Bible becomes essential. Opinion developed from the rapid reading of a text leads to faulty conclusions. Proper analysis leading to a correct interpretation is the only road to the understanding that leads to spiritual growth.

> Interpretation is not necessarily a separate step from observation, for often, as you carefully observe the text, at that very moment you begin to see what it means. Thus, interpretation flows out of observation.[19] Kay Arthur

---

[19] Kay Arthur, *How to Study Your Bible*, © 1994 by Precept Ministries,

Appropriate interpretation using close scrutiny of the text leads to the accurate understanding of the truth of Scripture. Detailed observation is rewarded with the knowledge that leads to wisdom.

One essential in clarification is the use of cross-references. As interpretive experts have said many times, "Let Scripture interpret Scripture." The best tool we have for interpretation is the Bible itself.

Cross-references are verses or sections of Scripture that say or mean virtually the same thing. They are found everywhere in the Bible and lend credibility to the Word and to its author the Holy Spirit. God's Spirit is our guide in helping us to reveal the meaning of a text and He will remind us of other places where we have read or seen similar scriptures.

1 Corinthians 2:12-14 says this about the Holy Spirit as our source of understanding God's Word," "*Now we have received, not the spirit of the world, but the Spirit who is from God, so that we may know the things freely given to us by God, which things we also speak, not in words taught by human wisdom, but in those taught by the Spirit, combining spiritual thoughts with spiritual words. But a natural man does not accept the things of the Spirit of God, for they are foolishness to him; and he cannot understand them, because they are spiritually appraised.*"

Interpretation, then, is the most important element in Bible study. Resolving textual or contextual issues allows us to understand what the scripture means. Before we can apply it to our lives we must know what God is trying to tell us.

Harvest House Publishers, Eugene, OR, 97402, p. 12

Context

Context is important to interpretation since it tells us what a specific word, verse, or paragraph means in relation to the whole Bible. God has one thought stream throughout the Bible from its beginning in Genesis to its end in Revelation. His purpose could be summarized as redemption through the transformation of Mankind.

> *Therefore, if anyone is in Christ, he is a new creature; the old things passed away; behold, new things have come* (2 Corinthians 5:17).

> *He forgives all my sins and heals all my diseases. who redeems your life from the pit and crowns you with love and compassion* (Psalm 103:3-4).

God's desires for us to know Him through His Son Jesus. In Philippians 3:10, Paul says this about knowing Jesus, "*I want to know Christ--yes, to know the power of his resurrection and participation in his sufferings, and so, somehow, attaining to the resurrection from the dead.*" "*...to know the power of His resurrection*" means becoming like him in his death.

Context helps us to know His love and acceptance for those who believe in Him. 1 Peter 3:9 says, "*The Lord is not slow in keeping his promise, as some understand slowness. Instead, he is patient with you, not wanting anyone to perish, but everyone to come to repentance.*" But also, He detests sin and those who won't believe (Proverbs 6:6-19). We see this thread throughout the Bible. This one complex but undeniable description provides the context for everything we read.

This one phrase, redemption through transformation, explains God's love for Adam and Eve and His punishment for their sin. It describes His patience and longsuffering walk with Israel. It defines the plan of God for the salvation of mankind. Only God could make the sacrifice that was necessary to justify sin and provide a way for mankind to receive eternal life.

Therefore, atonement allows us to understand the birth, life, beatings, death, resurrection, and ascension of His Son Jesus that provided for spiritual metamorphosis. It is the only way that we can adequately discern the words of the epistles that lay out the directions for our salvation and spiritual growth.

Finally, the truth of redemption is the only way that we can fully understand the Book of Revelation that shows His reward for belief and judgment for unbelief.

Speed:

As we discussed earlier, speed can be the enemy of interpretation. Reading a chapter or book just to get through it is not the way to understand scripture. There must be time for contemplation. It is during this time of reflection that we receive discernment. As we focus on the words of a verse, for example, the Spirit of God will help us with the understanding. Then, He will provide the wisdom that is a byproduct of interpretation.

Including Others:

One of the best ways to study God's Word is with another person or in a group. Study habits are difficult to establish and even more challenging to maintain. The best way to assure that we manage our study time is to get others involved. Accountability is vital to maintaining a rigorous, productive study program.

Being involved in a study with your spouse is a good alternative to a group study. Spousal studies allow both of you to grow in the same direction and at the same speed. Obedience to the scripture becomes easier when we have an accountability partner. This is especially true when we study with our spouse. **The family that studies together, grows together**!

Being in an Organized Small Group:

Another way to grow in knowledge and wisdom is to be part of a structured church small group or an organized local or national denominational or interdenominational Bible study. Making that commitment encourages us to study the material for the next week. The study will reveal new ways to view the Bible as well as help with the interpretation of sections of scripture. However, the added importance of the group dynamic will allow us to ask questions when we are uncertain of an interpretation and get feedback from the group.

Peer pressure becomes the incentive to remain involved on a regular basis as we try to keep up with the others. Groups like these mentioned, are an excellent way to hold yourself accountable for growth.

Paying attention in Church:

Pastors continually interpret scripture as they preach and teach God's Word. When we listen closely to what is said, we will hear various interpretations of words and verses with which we may or may not be familiar. Growing can come from listening. Taking notes and later copying them into the computer or placing them in the appropriate file folder allows for future studies.

Many Christians resist organized religion today due to a bad experience that they had in church either while growing up or previously as an adult. Churches that are more social clubs than they are places of worship and teaching tend to form clicks and are more interested in impressing others with worldly possessions and accomplishments than being serious students of the Bible. However, most churches are serious about growing spiritually and offer a variety of programs to help their members and attendees learn about the Scriptures.

God wants us to be in a group setting where we can learn from others who are farther along on their spiritual journey. The Bible tells us in Hebrews 10:24-25 to *"consider how we may spur one another on toward love and good deeds, not giving up meeting together, as some are in the habit of doing, but encouraging one another-- and all the more as you see the Day approaching."* God will provide a safe place for worship and quality teaching.

Journaling:

Taking notes has always been invaluable to me. Once we have taken notes, we can either type the notes into the computer or scan them in and put them in files according to topic or location. Then, when we have a question about a word, verse, or section of Scripture, we can open those files and have access to the notes that have been taken. Purchasing a Bible with large margins and deep inside gutter is also helpful for taking notes. In that way, the notes are easily accessible as we are studying.

Finding a Mentor:

Mentoring others is an often forgotten or overlooked option. Seeking a mentor means finding someone who is well versed in the scripture with years of interpretive experience, Bible knowledge, and wisdom from the Spirit's teaching. Meeting on a regular basis with a mentor will provide valuable insight into God's word.

Outside Resources: Using Historically Accepted Extra-Biblical Tools

In addition, we should use commentaries and other written and oral research tools which have proven over time to be a truthful and accurate interpretation of the Word of God.

Using outside resources for interpretation or study is important. There are many books that can be purchased, however, there are great resources online. The most productive way to use the internet for Bible study is to type in a verse location like Romans 5:1 and behind it type the word "commentary or commentaries." You will find pages of entries that will provide excellent information. However, be careful to choose those that are fundamental and evangelical.

For a bibliography of the websites that can be used for solid Bible teaching see

Appendix B: *Recommended commentaries and authors*

The Author, Setting, Purpose, and Point

These important areas of research are about the scripture being studied. As a result. they are critical to understanding the underlying structure and content of the writing itself.

1. The Author:

> God could have simply dictated His Word through one man or maintained a consistent tone and vocabulary across several human authors. Instead...He worked through a diverse collection of authors and personalities to deliver His Word to His people, without sacrificing the continuity or character of Scripture.[20] – John MacArthur

Naturally, as we know from God's Word, the author of all scripture is the Holy Spirit (2 Timothy 3:16-17). However, each person that the Spirit chose to write the Scripture is unique.

Mosses could have been the Pharaoh but instead followed God's plan for his life and lead Israel out of Egypt (Hebrews 11:23-28). Isaiah was "a man of unclean lips" until God purified them with a coal from the alter providing atonement for his sin and transformed him into a Prophet to Israel (Isaiah 6:5-7). Daniel was just a young boy when he was taken up into captivity by Nebuchadnezzar to Babylon (Daniel 1:1-7).

Matthew was a tax collector, hated by the Jews when Jesus chose him to be an Apostle (Matthew 9:9). Paul was responsible for Christians being persecuted, jailed, and even killed before Jesus redeemed him on the road to Damascus (Acts 22:1-21). These are only a few of the examples of the interesting and controversial people that God chose as writers for the Bible.

---

[20] John MacArthur, *How did God Guide the Biblical Writers*, © Grace to You, All Rights Reserved, gty.org/library/blog/B160715/how-did-god-guide-the-biblical-writers

2. The Setting:

> The geography of the Bible is a rich and intricate field of study. Putting the text of the Bible into context can be a complicated affair as the Bible spans several thousand years. As ruling empires changed, so did place names and geographical boundaries. As a result, places in the Bible often have numerous names or variant language and spellings.[21]

You should go to Israel. I am not a travel agent, or a parachurch organization, or a church attempting to sell a trip package. However, I have been in Israel and Jordan twice and I am saying every Christian should go there. There is nothing like seeing the land that God gave to Israel and its surrounding countries to receive a true picture of how important the settings are to the accounts of God's Word. To stand on Mount Nebo where God showed Moses the promised land but did not allow him to enter is breathtaking.

To see the ruins of Jericho and the walls that are laying outward is thrilling. To look down into the Valley of the Shadow of Death along the road from Jericho to Jerusalem mentioned in Psalm 23 and the account of the good Samaritan take us back centuries.

To see Jerusalem, it's wall, the wailing wall, the pool of Bethesda where Jesus healed the blind man is awe inspiring. The birthplace of Jesus, the tomb where he was buried, Mount Olivet, the Mount of Ascension, I

---

[21] The Lands of the Bible—A Thematic Guide, © 2018. All Rights

could go on and on. Israel is unique. The settings in the Bible are essential to the understanding of Scripture as a whole.

> ...we know the whole world is His, yet this one parcel of land on the earth has a unique relationship to Him. About Israel, He says, "The land, moreover, shall not be sold permanently, for the land is Mine: for you are but aliens and sojourners with Me" (Leviticus 25:23).[22] – Clarence H. Wagner Jr.

3. <u>The Purpose</u>:

God's purpose, His reason for doing anything and everything, is expressed in many ways, but it never varies. As we mentioned, God's purpose is redemption. The justification of believers in the action of salvation, referred to as the *"washing of regeneration,* initiates metamorphoses (Titus 3:5). Spiritual growth is ongoing transformation (Romans 12:2).

God's Purpose for Transformation: *"But I have raised you up for this very purpose, that I might show you my power and that my name might be proclaimed in all the earth"* (Exodus 9:16).

God's Purpose cannot be Thwarted: *"I know that you can do all things; no purpose of yours can be thwarted"* (Job 42:2).

God's Purpose for Believers: *"Therefore, my dear*

Reserved, oxfordbiblicalstudies.com/resource/biblelands.xhtml
[22] Clarence H. Wagner, Jr., *12 Keys to Understanding Israel in the Bible*, no copyright listed, ldolphin.org/twelvekeys.html.

friends, as you have always obeyed--not only in my presence, but now much more in my absence--continue to work out your salvation with fear and trembling, for it is God who works in you to will and to act in order to fulfill his good purpose, for it is God who works in you to will and to act in order to fulfill his good purpose (Philippians 2:12-13).

God Works all things to His Purpose: *"And we know that in all things God works for the good of those who love him, who have been called according to his purpose"* (Romans 8:28).

4. The Point:

A point is the important or essential thing.[23] A biblical purpose and the biblical point may seem to be the same thing. However, the purpose is result of an action while the point is the reasoning behind an action.

The purpose for Jesus going to the cross was the action of providing redemption. The reason or point of the cross was that God had to provide the perfect sacrifice to provide reparation. The point is the reasoning behind the action and the purpose is what is achieved by the completion of the action.

Colossians 1:9 says, *"For this reason, since the day we heard about you, we have not stopped praying for you. We continually ask God to fill you with the knowledge of his will through all the wisdom and understanding that*

---

[23] Point, The American Heritage® Idioms Dictionary Copyright © 2002, 2001, 1995 by Houghton Mifflin Harcourt Publishing Company. Published by Houghton Mifflin Harcourt Publishing Company, dictionary.com/browse/point?s=t.

the Spirit gives." The point of verse or the reason for Paul's prayer was that they had heard about the disciples living in Colossi. Since they were believers, they would need prayer. The purpose of the prayer was to provide God's wisdom and understanding through the Holy Spirit.

Paraphrasing the Word

Read a book of the Bible. Then, starting with the first chapter, write out each verse or section of verses in a common sense language. This will help make sense of the wording of each verse.

Here is an example using 1 Timothy 1:1

<u>Original Verse</u>: *"Paul, an apostle of Christ Jesus by the command of God our Savior and of Christ Jesus our hope"* (1 Timothy 1:1 NIV).

<u>Personal Paraphrase</u>: Paul, called and assigned to be an Apostle by Jesus himself, who is the One who saves us, being obedient to the instructions of God, and of this same Christ Jesus who is our hope.

This paraphrase is an interpretation of the verse. This explanatory rewording of the verse now becomes a basis for digging deeper into various authorities to verify the validity of the paraphrase.

When do We Study the Bible?

Getting it Right and Starting it Right Now

1. <u>The Best Time to Study</u>:

　　The best time to study the Bible is when our minds are the most alert. For many people that is the first thing in the morning. The morning meets the requirement of putting God first in our lives. At the same time, it meets the requirement of giving God the best of everything if morning is the best time of the day. 2 Timothy 2:15 tells us to "*Do your best to present yourself to God as an approved worker who has nothing to be ashamed of, handling the word of truth with precision.*"

2. <u>The Study Plan</u>:

　　Having a planned study, even if it is our own plan and not pre-packaged, will facilitate and accelerate study effectiveness.

3. <u>The Length of Time to Study</u>:

　　How much time do we need to put in to our study plan for it to be effective? I would say that an hour of actual study would be a minimum to provide adequate time to get deeply into a word or verse. That does not include the time it takes to get dressed and to fix coffee and breakfast.

4. <u>Scheduling the Time to Study</u>:

>The past is gone and cannot be changed. The future is something that can be planned but not controlled. People can only live in the "now." The present is where time is controlled. To get into a positive habit of study, the person needs to calendar their time.

Two Agents for controlling time:

1. <u>Get God involved</u>:

>God does not live within time; He invented it.

>God is not constrained by time; He knows the future.

>God wants our time; He desires, blesses, and multiplies it.

>"God multiplies whatever we give to him. If you give God your time, he multiplies it.[24]
>– Rick Warren

2. <u>Prioritize It</u>: Not just prioritizing the activities and events that capture time, but prioritizing time itself.

Here are the priorities for our time according to Scripture:

<u>God</u>: Prayer and the Study of God's Word (2 Timothy 2:15), attending church (Hebrews 10:25), worshipping God (Psalm 110:2-5), and working for God (Matthew 28:19-20, Ephesians 2:10).

Family: Quality family time is essential to maintaining a Christian home (Proverbs 22:6, 1 Peter 3:1 and 7, Ephesians 6:1, Colossians 3:20, and Ephesians 6:4).

3. Work: The worker needs to be worthy of the wages they are paid (1 Timothy 5:18 and Luke 10:7).

4. Recreation and Rest: (Genesis 2:2-3, Exodus 20:9-10, Psalm 23:1-3, Isaiah 57:2, Matthew 11:28-30, Mark 6:31, and Hebrews 4:9-11).

Put Time into in blocks on the calendar. There are 112 waking hours in a week, take those hours and put them in blocks representing different levels of priorities. Use a weekly planner and block out time for God, then family time, then the work schedule, and finally the time for recreation, rest, and relaxation.

Momentum is motivation on steroids

Once the believer is motivated to reach a new level of *Managing Their Life and Taking Control their Time*, momentum kicks in and the spiritual growth that maturing believers seek is assured. The quality of effort during any day is of greater importance than the quantity of time. We must plan our time well and establish routines that emphasize the quality of time spent. Plan and prepare for quality.

> "The fact of the matter is, if all that activity isn't taking you where you want to go, then it's just wasted time."[25] – Stanley, Joiner, Jones

---

[24] Rick Warren, Controlling Your Time, Public Domain, Saddleback Seminar, Irvine, CA, 2016.
[25] Andy Stanley, Reggie Joiner, Lane Jones, Practices of effective Ministry, Multnomah Publishers, sister, Oregon. P.36

Summary

When we squander time, we are losing the very substance that makes up life.

> "Your life is the sum result of all the choices you make, both consciously and unconsciously. If you can control the process of choosing, you can take control of all aspects of your life. You can find the freedom that comes from being in charge of yourself."[26] – Robert F. Bennett
>
> Proverbs 3:5-6 (NASB), *"Trust in the Lord with all your heart and do not lean on your own understanding. In all your ways acknowledge Him, and He will make your paths straight."*

5. <u>Bonus Study Time</u>: Bonus study time is any break during the day when we are waiting for the next assignment or appointment. It may be the fifteen-minute break at work that we are given by law each day in the morning and in the afternoon. We could be waiting for a return phone call. Whenever we have spare time we could turn that time into productive study time.

    If there is no computer available, the smartphone can become our Bible, our research tool, and our journal. There are apps for everything. A good way to do a quick study would be to follow these simple steps.

---

[26] Robert Forest Bennett, brainyquote.com/quotes/quotes/r/robertfost130327.html

Do this for Growth:

Pray: Pray for God's help and direction.

Open the App: Open your bible app (ESV Bible is free and a good App since it allows for all the modern translations). Locate a verse that is being studied or a new one to be studied.

Read: Read a verse or a section of Scripture.

Copy: Copy that Scripture and paste it in the "notes" app. Now you have a journal for your study.

Paste: Paste the verse to your "Note App."

Rewrite: After reading the Scripture that has been chosen, rewrite it in a language that interprets what it is saying.

Search: Use your search engine (Google, Firefox, Bing, Explorer, etc.) to do research on the verse to help better understand what others have gleaned from the verse. Copy and paste those words and phrases into your journal entry. Rewrite the original thoughts adding any new ideas received from the research reviewed.

Email it: When the journal entry is finished, copy and paste it to your email address and send the finished study to yourself.

Copy and Paste to a Word Document: Later, the email can be opened, copied and pasted to a word document on your computer.

<u>Save to a Doc File Folder</u>: Once the study has been copied to a Word document, save it to as a document (doc) on your hard drive or desktop.

<u>Print</u>: Print a hard copy if you are keeping a notebook or notes in a file folder.

Bible study can be done anywhere, anytime. Anytime is a good time for studying God's Word.

Where do we Study the Bible?

The simple answer to this question is anywhere. However, to maintain our goal of remembering what we have studied for the future, we would also need access to a Bible or device that has a Bible and writing tools or a device that allows us to record what we have discovered in our study.

There are some conditions that are better than others for Bible study. For the best study conditions, consider the following recommendations:

1. <u>Quiet</u>: Finding a place to study where there are diminished distractions allows us to maintain the mental state of concentration needed to study God's Word.

2. <u>Good Lighting</u>: a well-lit location will keep us from getting drowsy. Tired eyes are generally a result of squinting in inadequate light.

3. <u>Access to a Variety of Tools</u>: We should always plan to have easy access to all the tools we need for our study. If all the study aids are systematically arranged and kept in one location, it saves time and frustration in locating the exact piece of information needed.

4. <u>Ample Time</u>: even though we can study the Scripture

anywhere and at any time, it is best if ample time for reflection and note taking is prearranged.

5. <u>Solitary Confinement</u>: Asking others not to bother us unless it is an emergency is a good way to plan for quiet and to teach others to respect planned downtime.

Closing Thoughts

Don't wait for the right time to study God's word. As the commercials say, "Just do it!" Procrastination is the bane of mankind. It was Charles Dickens that said, "My advice is to never do tomorrow what you can do today. Procrastination is the thief of time."[27] From a biblical perspective, Colossians 3:23-24 has both a command and a promise, *"Whatever you do, work at it with all your heart, as working for the Lord, not for human masters since you know that you will receive an inheritance from the Lord as a reward. It is the Lord Christ you are serving."*

There are many reasons to wait for the ideal time and place to study the Scriptures. However, according to Geoffrey Chaucer, "Time and tide wait for no man."[28] Nothing should stand in the way of seeking to know more about God's Word. The best time and place to start is now.

---

[27] Charles Dickens, *"David Copperfield"*, public domain, planetebook.com/free-ebooks/david-copperfield.pdf, p.160.
[28] What does Time and Tide Waits for no Man Mean? © copyright 2003-2018 Study.com. All other trademarks and copyrights are the property of their respective owners. All rights reserved.
study.com/academy/answer/what-does-time-and-tide-wait-for-no-man-mean.html

Notes

Appendix A: Navigator's One Year Bible Reading Plan

The Discipleship Journal Bible Reading Plan

The Discipleship Journal® Bible Reading Plan

The *Discipleship Journal* Bible Reading Plan offers special features that will aid you in your journey through the Bible.

- By reading from four separate places in the Scriptures every day, you should be able to better grasp the unity of the Scriptures, as well as enjoy the variety of four different viewpoints.

- You can begin at any point during the year.

- To prevent the frustration of falling behind, which most of us tend to do when following a Bible reading plan, each month of this plan gives you only 25 readings. Since you'll have several "free days" each month, you could set aside Sundays either not to read at all or to catch up on any readings you may have missed in the past week.

- If you finish the month's readings by the twenty-fifth, you could use the final days of the month to study the passages that challenged or intrigued you.

- If reading through the entire Bible in one year looms as too large a task, you can alter the plan to meet your needs. For example, you could read the gospels and the wisdom books this year, and the other two categories next year.

In the year ahead, ask God each day to speak directly to you from the Scripture portions you read. Be expectant, and let your continual exposure to God's Word reshape your attitudes and behavior as you gain a better understanding of every part of His written testimony to us.

(DJ) Discipleship Journal®
HELPING YOU GROW IN CHRIST

To **subscribe**, go to www.discipleshipjournal.com
Or call: 1-800-877-1811 | Or write: P.O. Box 5545, Harlan, IA 51593-1048

NAVPRESS
Discipleship Inside Out™

Permission is granted to download and print one copy to use.
ISBN 978-1-57683-974-4
© 2005 by The Navigators. All rights reserved.
To order copies of this resource, see www.navpress.com.

The Discipleship Journal Bible Reading Plan

January

New Testament		Old Testament	
▸ MATTHEW	▸ ACTS	▸ PSALMS	▸ GENESIS
1. ☐ 1:1-17	☐ 1:1-11	☐ 1	☐ 1-2
2. ☐ 1:18-25	☐ 1:12-26	☐ 2	☐ 3-4
3. ☐ 2:1-12	☐ 2:1-21	☐ 3	☐ 5-6
4. ☐ 2:13-23	☐ 2:22-47	☐ 4	☐ 9-11
5. ☐ 3:1-12	☐ 3	☐ 5	☐ 12-14
6. ☐ 3:13-17	☐ 4:1-22	☐ 6	☐ 15-17
7. ☐ 4:1-11	☐ 4:23-37	☐ 7	☐ 18-20
8. ☐ 4:12-17	☐ 5:1-16	☐ 8	☐ 21-23
9. ☐ 4:18-25	☐ 5:17-42	☐ 9	☐ 24
10. ☐ 5:1-12	☐ 6	☐ 10	☐ 25-26
11. ☐ 5:13-20	☐ 7:1-38	☐ 11	☐ 27-28
12. ☐ 5:21-32	☐ 7:39-60	☐ 12	☐ 29-30
13. ☐ 5:33-48	☐ 8:1-25	☐ 13	☐ 31
14. ☐ 6:1-18	☐ 8:26-40	☐ 14	☐ 32-33
15. ☐ 6:19-24	☐ 9:1-19	☐ 15	☐ 34-35
16. ☐ 6:25-34	☐ 9:20-43	☐ 16	☐ 36
17. ☐ 7:1-14	☐ 10:1-23	☐ 17	☐ 37-38
18. ☐ 7:15-29	☐ 10:24-48	☐ 18:1-24	☐ 39-40
19. ☐ 8:1-13	☐ 11:1-18	☐ 18:25-50	☐ 41
20. ☐ 8:14-22	☐ 11:19-30	☐ 19	☐ 42-43
21. ☐ 8:23-34	☐ 12	☐ 20	☐ 44-45
22. ☐ 9:1-13	☐ 13:1-25	☐ 21	☐ 46-47
23. ☐ 9:14-26	☐ 13:26-52	☐ 22:1-11	☐ 48
24. ☐ 9:27-38	☐ 14	☐ 22:12-31	☐ 49
25. ☐ 10:1-20	☐ 15:1-21	☐ 23	☐ 50

February

New Testament		Old Testament	
▸ MATTHEW	▸ ACTS	▸ PSALMS	▸ EXODUS
1. ☐ 10:21-42	☐ 15:22-41	☐ 24	☐ 1-3
2. ☐ 11:1-19	☐ 16:1-15	☐ 25	☐ 4-6
3. ☐ 11:20-30	☐ 16:16-40	☐ 26	☐ 7-9
4. ☐ 12:1-21	☐ 17:1-15	☐ 27	☐ 10-12
5. ☐ 12:22-37	☐ 17:16-34	☐ 28	☐ 13-15
6. ☐ 12:38-50	☐ 18:1-17	☐ 29	☐ 16-18
7. ☐ 13:1-23	☐ 18:18-28	☐ 30	☐ 19-20
8. ☐ 13:24-43	☐ 19:1-22	☐ 31	☐ 21-23
9. ☐ 13:44-58	☐ 19:23-41	☐ 32	☐ 24-26
10. ☐ 14:1-21	☐ 20:1-12	☐ 33	☐ 27-29
11. ☐ 14:22-36	☐ 20:13-38	☐ 34	☐ 30-31
12. ☐ 15:1-20	☐ 21:1-26	☐ 35	☐ 32-33
13. ☐ 15:21-39	☐ 21:27-40	☐ 36	☐ 34
14. ☐ 16:1-12	☐ 22	☐ 37:1-22	☐ 35-37
15. ☐ 16:13-28	☐ 23:1-11	☐ 37:23-40	☐ 38-40
			▸ LEVITICUS
16. ☐ 17:1-13	☐ 23:12-35	☐ 38	☐ 1-4
17. ☐ 17:14-27	☐ 24	☐ 39	☐ 5-7
18. ☐ 18:1-14	☐ 25:1-12	☐ 40	☐ 8-10
19. ☐ 18:15-35	☐ 25:13-27	☐ 41	☐ 11-13
20. ☐ 19:1-15	☐ 26:1-18	☐ 42	☐ 14-15
21. ☐ 19:16-30	☐ 26:19-32	☐ 43	☐ 16-17
22. ☐ 20:1-16	☐ 27:1-26	☐ 44	☐ 18-20
23. ☐ 20:17-34	☐ 27:27-44	☐ 45	☐ 21-23
24. ☐ 21:1-11	☐ 28:1-16	☐ 46	☐ 24-25
25. ☐ 21:12-22	☐ 28:17-31	☐ 47	☐ 26-27

March

New Testament		Old Testament	
▸ MATTHEW	▸ ROMANS	▸ PSALMS	▸ NUMBERS
1. ☐ 21:23-32	☐ 1:1-17	☐ 48	☐ 1-2
2. ☐ 21:33-46	☐ 1:18-32	☐ 49	☐ 3-4
3. ☐ 22:1-14	☐ 2	☐ 50	☐ 5-6
4. ☐ 22:15-33	☐ 3	☐ 51	☐ 7-8
5. ☐ 22:34-46	☐ 4	☐ 52	☐ 9-11
6. ☐ 23:1-12	☐ 5:1-11	☐ 53	☐ 12-14
7. ☐ 23:13-24	☐ 5:12-21	☐ 54	☐ 15-17
8. ☐ 23:25-39	☐ 6:1-14	☐ 55	☐ 18-20
9. ☐ 24:1-14	☐ 6:15-23	☐ 56	☐ 21-22
10. ☐ 24:15-35	☐ 7:1-12	☐ 57	☐ 23-25
11. ☐ 24:36-51	☐ 7:13-25	☐ 58	☐ 26-27
12. ☐ 25:1-13	☐ 8:1-17	☐ 59	☐ 28-30
13. ☐ 25:14-30	☐ 8:18-39	☐ 60	☐ 31-32
14. ☐ 25:31-46	☐ 9:1-18	☐ 61	☐ 33-36
			▸ DEUT.
15. ☐ 26:1-16	☐ 9:19-33	☐ 62	☐ 1-3
16. ☐ 26:17-35	☐ 10	☐ 63	☐ 4-5
17. ☐ 26:36-56	☐ 11:1-24	☐ 64	☐ 6-8
18. ☐ 26:57-75	☐ 11:25-36	☐ 65	☐ 9-12
19. ☐ 27:1-10	☐ 12:1-8	☐ 66	☐ 13-17
20. ☐ 27:11-26	☐ 12:9-21	☐ 67	☐ 18-21
21. ☐ 27:27-44	☐ 13	☐ 68	☐ 22-26
22. ☐ 27:45-56	☐ 14	☐ 69:1-18	☐ 27-28
23. ☐ 27:57-66	☐ 15:1-13	☐ 69:19-36	☐ 29-31
24. ☐ 28:1-10	☐ 15:14-33	☐ 70	☐ 32
25. ☐ 28:11-20	☐ 16	☐ 71	☐ 33-34

April

New Testament		Old Testament	
▸ MARK	▸ 1 COR.	▸ PSALMS	▸ JOSHUA
1. ☐ 1:1-8	☐ 1:1-17	☐ 72	☐ 1-2
2. ☐ 1:9-20	☐ 1:18-31	☐ 73	☐ 3-5
3. ☐ 1:21-34	☐ 2	☐ 74	☐ 6-7
4. ☐ 1:35-45	☐ 3	☐ 75	☐ 8-9
5. ☐ 2:1-12	☐ 4	☐ 76	☐ 10-12
6. ☐ 2:13-17	☐ 5	☐ 77	☐ 13-14
7. ☐ 2:18-28	☐ 6:1-11	☐ 78:1-39	☐ 15-17
8. ☐ 3:1-19	☐ 6:12-20	☐ 78:40-72	☐ 18-19
9. ☐ 3:20-35	☐ 7:1-16	☐ 79	☐ 20-21
10. ☐ 4:1-20	☐ 7:17-40	☐ 80	☐ 22-23
11. ☐ 4:21-41	☐ 8	☐ 81	☐ 24
			▸ JUDGES
12.			☐ 1-3
13. ☐ 5:1-20	☐ 9:1-12	☐ 82	☐ 4-5
14. ☐ 5:21-43	☐ 9:13-27	☐ 83	☐ 6-7
15. ☐ 6:1-13	☐ 10:1-13	☐ 84	☐ 8
16. ☐ 6:14-29	☐ 10:14-33	☐ 85	☐ 9
17. ☐ 6:30-44	☐ 11:1-16	☐ 86	☐ 10-12
18. ☐ 6:45-56	☐ 11:17-34	☐ 87	☐ 13-15
19. ☐ 7:1-23	☐ 12:1-13	☐ 88	☐ 16
20. ☐ 7:24-37	☐ 12:14-31	☐ 89:1-18	☐ 17-18
21. ☐ 8:1-21	☐ 13	☐ 89:19-52	☐ 19
22. ☐ 8:22-30	☐ 14:1-25	☐ 90	☐ 20-21
			▸ RUTH
23. ☐ 8:31-38	☐ 14:26-40	☐ 91	☐ 1
24. ☐ 9:1-13	☐ 15:1-28	☐ 92	☐ 2-3
25. ☐ 9:14-32	☐ 15:29-58	☐ 93	☐ 4
	☐ 16	☐ 94	

The Discipleship Journal Bible Reading Plan

	New Testament		Old Testament			New Testament		Old Testament	
	▸ MARK	▸ 2 COR.	▸ PSALMS	▸ 1 SAMUEL		▸ LUKE	▸ EPHESIANS	▸ PSALMS	▸ 1 KINGS
1.	☐ 9:33-50	☐ 1:1-11	☐ 95	☐ 1-2	1.	☐ 1:1-25	☐ 1:1-14	☐ 119:1-8	☐ 1
2.	☐ 10:1-16	☐ 1:12-24	☐ 96	☐ 3-5	2.	☐ 1:26-38	☐ 1:15-23	☐ 119:9-16	☐ 2-3
3.	☐ 10:17-34	☐ 2	☐ 97	☐ 6-8	3.	☐ 1:39-56	☐ 2:1-10	☐ 119:17-24	☐ 4-5
4.	☐ 10:35-52	☐ 3	☐ 98	☐ 9-10	4.	☐ 1:57-66	☐ 2:11-22	☐ 119:25-32	☐ 6-7
5.	☐ 11:1-11	☐ 4	☐ 99	☐ 11-13	5.	☐ 1:67-80	☐ 3:1-13	☐ 119:33-40	☐ 8
6.	☐ 11:12-26	☐ 5	☐ 100	☐ 14	6.	☐ 2:1-20	☐ 3:14-21	☐ 119:41-48	☐ 9-10
7.	☐ 11:27-33	☐ 6	☐ 101	☐ 15-16	7.	☐ 2:21-40	☐ 4:1-16	☐ 119:49-56	☐ 11
8.	☐ 12:1-12	☐ 7	☐ 102	☐ 17-18	8.	☐ 2:41-52	☐ 4:17-24	☐ 119:57-64	☐ 12
9.	☐ 12:13-27	☐ 8	☐ 103	☐ 19-20	9.	☐ 3:1-20	☐ 4:25-32	☐ 119:65-72	☐ 13-14
10.	☐ 12:28-34	☐ 9	☐ 104	☐ 21-23	10.	☐ 3:21-38	☐ 5:1-21	☐ 119:73-80	☐ 15-16
11.	☐ 12:35-44	☐ 10	☐ 105	☐ 24-25	11.	☐ 4:1-12	☐ 5:22-33	☐ 119:81-88	☐ 17-18
12.	☐ 13:1-13	☐ 11:1-15	☐ 106:1-23	☐ 26-28	12.	☐ 4:13-30	☐ 6:1-9	☐ 119:89-96	☐ 19-20
13.	☐ 13:14-31	☐ 11:16-33	☐ 106:24-48	☐ 29-31	13.	☐ 4:31-37	☐ 6:10-24	☐ 119:97-104	☐ 21-22
				▸ 2 SAMUEL			▸ PHILIPPIANS		▸ 2 KINGS
14.	☐ 13:32-37	☐ 12:1-10	☐ 107	☐ 1-2	14.	☐ 4:38-44	☐ 1:1-11	☐ 119:105-112	☐ 1-3
15.	☐ 14:1-11	☐ 12:11-21	☐ 108	☐ 3-4	15.	☐ 5:1-11	☐ 1:12-20	☐ 119:113-120	☐ 4-5
16.	☐ 14:12-31	☐ 13	☐ 109	☐ 5-7	16.	☐ 5:12-16	☐ 1:21-30	☐ 119:121-128	☐ 6-7
		▸ GALATIANS			17.	☐ 5:17-26	☐ 2:1-11	☐ 119:129-136	☐ 8-9
17.	☐ 14:32-42	☐ 1	☐ 110	☐ 8-10	18.	☐ 5:27-32	☐ 2:12-18	☐ 119:137-144	☐ 10-11
18.	☐ 14:43-52	☐ 2	☐ 111	☐ 11-12	19.	☐ 5:33-39	☐ 2:19-30	☐ 119:145-152	☐ 12-13
19.	☐ 14:53-65	☐ 3:1-14	☐ 112	☐ 13	20.	☐ 6:1-16	☐ 3:1-9	☐ 119:153-160	☐ 14-15
20.	☐ 14:66-72	☐ 3:15-29	☐ 113	☐ 14-15	21.	☐ 6:17-26	☐ 3:10-14	☐ 119:161-168	☐ 16-17
21.	☐ 15:1-15	☐ 4:1-20	☐ 114	☐ 16-17	22.	☐ 6:27-36	☐ 3:15-21	☐ 119:169-176	☐ 18-19
22.	☐ 15:16-32	☐ 4:21-31	☐ 115	☐ 18-19	23.	☐ 6:37-42	☐ 4:1-7	☐ 120	☐ 20-21
23.	☐ 15:33-41	☐ 5:1-12	☐ 116	☐ 20-21	24.	☐ 6:43-49	☐ 4:8-13	☐ 121	☐ 22-23
24.	☐ 15:42-47	☐ 5:13-26	☐ 117	☐ 22	25.	☐ 7:1-10	☐ 4:14-23	☐ 122	☐ 24-25
25.	☐ 16	☐ 6	☐ 118	☐ 23-24					

	New Testament		Old Testament			New Testament		Old Testament	
	▸ LUKE	▸ COLOSSIANS	▸ PSALMS	▸ 1 CHRON.		▸ LUKE	▸ 1 TIMOTHY	▸ PROVERBS	▸ EZRA
1.	☐ 7:11-17	☐ 1:1-14	☐ 123-124	☐ 1-2	1.	☐ 13:1-9	☐ 1:1-11	☐ 1	☐ 1-2
2.	☐ 7:18-35	☐ 1:15-29	☐ 125	☐ 3-4	2.	☐ 13:10-21	☐ 1:12-20	☐ 2	☐ 3
3.	☐ 7:36-50	☐ 2:1-7	☐ 126	☐ 5-6	3.	☐ 13:22-35	☐ 2	☐ 3	☐ 4-5
4.	☐ 8:1-15	☐ 2:8-15	☐ 127	☐ 7-9	4.	☐ 14:1-14	☐ 3:1-10	☐ 4	☐ 6
5.	☐ 8:16-25	☐ 2:16-23	☐ 128	☐ 10-11	5.	☐ 14:15-24	☐ 3:11-16	☐ 5	☐ 7
6.	☐ 8:26-39	☐ 3:1-14	☐ 129	☐ 12-14	6.	☐ 14:25-35	☐ 4	☐ 6	☐ 8
7.	☐ 8:40-56	☐ 3:15-25	☐ 130-131	☐ 15-16	7.	☐ 15:1-10	☐ 5:1-10	☐ 7	☐ 9
8.	☐ 9:1-17	☐ 4:1-9	☐ 132	☐ 17-19	8.	☐ 15:11-32	☐ 5:16-25	☐ 8	☐ 10
9.	☐ 9:18-27	☐ 4:10-18	☐ 133-134	☐ 20-22					▸ NEH.
		▸ 1 THESSALONIANS			9.	☐ 16:1-9	☐ 6:1-10	☐ 9	☐ 1-2
10.	☐ 9:28-36	☐ 1	☐ 135	☐ 23-26	10.	☐ 16:10-18	☐ 6:11-21	☐ 10:1-15	☐ 3
11.	☐ 9:37-50	☐ 2:1-9	☐ 136	☐ 26-28			▸ 2 TIMOTHY		
12.	☐ 9:51-62	☐ 2:10-20	☐ 137	☐ 29	11.	☐ 16:19-31	☐ 1:1-7	☐ 10:17-32	☐ 4-5
				▸ 2 CHRON.	12.	☐ 17:1-10	☐ 1:8-18	☐ 11:1-15	☐ 6
13.	☐ 10:1-16	☐ 3:1-5	☐ 138	☐ 1-2	13.	☐ 17:11-19	☐ 2:1-13	☐ 11:16-31	☐ 7
14.	☐ 10:17-24	☐ 3:7-13	☐ 139	☐ 3-5	14.	☐ 17:20-37	☐ 2:14-26	☐ 12:1-14	☐ 8
15.	☐ 10:25-37	☐ 4:1-10	☐ 140	☐ 6-7	15.	☐ 18:1-8	☐ 3:1-9	☐ 12:15-28	☐ 9
16.	☐ 10:38-42	☐ 4:11-18	☐ 141	☐ 8-9	16.	☐ 18:9-17	☐ 3:10-17	☐ 13:1-12	☐ 10
17.	☐ 11:1-13	☐ 5:1-11	☐ 142	☐ 10-12	17.	☐ 18:18-30	☐ 4	☐ 13:13-25	☐ 11
18.	☐ 11:14-28	☐ 5:12-28	☐ 143	☐ 13-16			▸ TITUS		
		▸ 2 THESSALONIANS			18.	☐ 18:31-43	☐ 1:1-9	☐ 14:1-18	☐ 12
19.	☐ 11:29-36	☐ 1:1-7	☐ 144	☐ 17-19	19.	☐ 19:1-10	☐ 1:10-16	☐ 14:19-35	☐ 13
20.	☐ 11:37-54	☐ 1:8-12	☐ 145	☐ 20-21					▸ ESTHER
21.	☐ 12:1-12	☐ 2:1-12	☐ 146	☐ 22-24	20.	☐ 19:11-27	☐ 2:1-10	☐ 15:1-17	☐ 1
22.	☐ 12:13-21	☐ 2:13-17	☐ 147	☐ 25-27	21.	☐ 19:28-38	☐ 2:11-15	☐ 15:18-33	☐ 2
23.	☐ 12:22-34	☐ 3:1-5	☐ 148	☐ 28-29	22.	☐ 19:39-48	☐ 3:1-8	☐ 16:1-16	☐ 3-4
24.	☐ 12:35-48	☐ 3:6-13	☐ 149	☐ 30-33	23.	☐ 20:1-8	☐ 3:9-15	☐ 16:17-33	☐ 5-6
25.	☐ 12:49-59	☐ 3:14-18	☐ 150	☐ 34-36			▸ PHILEMON		
					24.	☐ 20:9-19	☐ 1-11	☐ 17:1-14	☐ 7-8
					25.	☐ 20:20-26	☐ 12-25	☐ 17:15-28	☐ 9-10

ISBN 978-1-57683-974-4
© 2005 by The Navigators. All rights reserved. To order copies of this resource, see www.navpress.com.

74

The Discipleship Journal Bible Reading Plan

September

	New Testament		Old Testament	
	LUKE	HEBREWS	PROVERBS	ISAIAH
1.	20:27-40	1:1-9	18	1-2
2.	20:41-47	1:10-14	19:1-14	3-5
3.	21:1-19	2:1-9	19:15-29	6-8
4.	21:20-28	2:10-18	20:1-15	9-10
5.	21:29-38	3	20:16-30	11-13
6.	22:1-13	4:1-11	21:1-16	14-16
7.	22:14-23	4:12-16	21:17-31	17-20
8.	22:24-30	5	22:1-16	21-23
9.	22:31-38	6:1-12	22:17-29	24-26
10.	22:39-46	6:13-20	23:1-18	27-28
11.	22:47-53	7:1-10	23:19-35	29-30
12.	22:54-62	7:11-28	24:1-22	31-33
13.	22:63-71	8:1-6	24:23-34	34-36
14.	23:1-12	8:7-13	25:1-14	37-39
15.	23:13-25	9:1-10	25:15-28	40-41
16.	23:26-31	9:11-28	26:1-16	42-43
17.	23:32-37	10:1-18	26:17-28	44-45
18.	23:38-43	10:19-39	27:1-14	46-48
19.	23:44-49	11:1-16	27:15-27	49-50
20.	23:50-56	11:17-31	28:1-14	51-53
21.	24:1-12	11:32-40	28:15-28	54-55
22.	24:13-27	12:1-13	29:1-14	56-58
23.	24:28-35	12:14-29	29:15-27	59-61
24.	24:36-44	13:1-8	30	62-64
25.	24:45-53	13:9-25	31	65-66

October

	New Testament		Old Testament	
	JOHN	JAMES	ECCLES.	JEREMIAH
1.	1:1-18	1:1-11	1	1-2
2.	1:19-28	1:12-18	2:1-16	3-4
3.	1:29-34	1:19-27	2:17-26	5-6
4.	1:35-42	2:1-13	3:1-15	7-8
5.	1:43-51	2:14-26	3:16-22	10-11
6.	2:1-11	3:1-12	4	12-13
7.	2:12-25	3:13-18	5	14-15
8.	3:1-15	4:1-10	6	16-18
9.	3:16-21	4:11-17	7:1-14	19-22
10.	3:22-36	5:1-6	7:15-29	23-25
11.	4:1-14	5:7-12	8	26-29
12.	4:15-26	5:13-20	9	30-31
		1 PETER		
13.	4:27-42	1:1-9	10	32-34
14.	4:43-54	1:10-16	11	35-36
15.	5:1-15	1:17-25	12	37-40
			SONG OF SONGS	
16.	5:16-30	2:1-5	1	44-46
17.	5:31-47	2:9-17	2	47-48
18.	6:1-15	2:18-25	3	49
19.	6:16-24	3:1-7	4:1-7	50
20.	6:25-40	3:8-12	4:8-16	51
21.	6:41-59	3:13-22	5	52
				LAM.
22.	6:60-71	4:1-11	6	1
23.	7:1-13	4:12-19	7	2
24.	7:14-24	5:1-7	8:1-7	3
25.	7:25-36	5:8-14	8:8-14	4-5

November

	New Testament		Old Testament	
	JOHN	2 PETER	JOB	EZEKIEL
1.	7:37-44	1:1-11	1	1-3
2.	7:45-53	1:12-21	2	4-6
3.	8:1-11	2:1-9	3	9-12
4.	8:12-20	2:10-16	4	13-16
5.	8:21-30	2:17-22	5	18
6.	8:31-47	3:1-9	6	17-19
7.	8:48-59	3:10-18	7	20-21
		1 JOHN		
8.	9:1-12	1:1-4	8	22-23
9.	9:13-25	1:5-10	9:1-20	24-26
10.	9:26-41	2:1-11	9:21-35	27-28
11.	10:1-10	2:12-17	10	29-30
12.	10:11-21	2:18-23	11	31-32
13.	10:22-42	2:24-29	12	33-34
14.	11:1-16	3:1-10	13	35-36
15.	11:17-27	3:11-18	14	37-38
16.	11:28-44	3:19-24	15:1-16	40-41
17.	11:45-57	4:1-6	15:17-35	42-44
18.	12:1-11	4:7-21	16	45-47
19.	12:12-19	5:1-12	17	48
				DANIEL
20.	12:20-36	5:13-21	18	1-2
		2 JOHN		
21.	12:37-50	1-13	19	3-4
		3 JOHN		
22.	13:1-11	1-14	20	5-6
		JUDE		
23.	13:12-17	1-7	21:1-21	7-8
24.	13:18-30	8-16	21:22-34	9
25.	13:31-38	17-25	22	10-12

ISBN 978-1-57683-974-4
© 2006 by The Navigators. All rights reserved. To order copies of this resource, see www.navpress.com

December

	New Testament		Old Testament	
	JOHN	REVELATION	JOB	HOSEA
1.	14:1-14	1:1-8	23	1-3
2.	14:15-21	1:9-20	24	4-6
3.	14:22-31	2:1-17	25-26	7-8
4.	15:1-8	2:18-29	27	9-11
5.	15:9-17	3:1-13	28	13-14
				JOEL
6.	15:18-27	3:14-22	29	1
7.	16:1-11	4	30	2-3
				AMOS
8.	16:12-24	5	31:1-23	1-2
9.	16:25-33	6	31:24-40	3-4
10.	17:1-5	7	32	5-6
11.	17:6-19	8	33:1-11	7-9
				OBADIAH
12.	17:20-26	9	33:12-33	1-21
				JONAH
13.	18:1-18	10	34:1-20	1-4
				MICAH
14.	18:19-27	11	34:21-37	1-2
15.	18:28-40	12	35	4-5
16.	19:1-16	13	36:1-15	6-7
				NAHUM
17.	19:17-27	14	36:16-33	1-3
				HABAKKUK
18.	19:28-37	15	37	1-3
				ZEPHANIAH
19.	19:38-42	16	38:1-21	1-2
20.	20:1-9	17	38:22-41	3
				HAGGAI
21.	20:10-18	18	39	1-2
				ZECHARIAH
22.	20:19-23	19	40	1-5
23.	20:24-31	20	41:1-11	6-9
24.	21:1-14	21	41:12-34	10-14
				MALACHI
25.	21:15-25	22	42	1-4

Appendix B: Recommended commentaries and authors

If the web sites don't work, just type in the Bible verse or topic and type the person's name behind it. For example, if you are searching for information on the topic sanctification, type in sanctification Charles Spurgeon and everything he has said on sanctification will appear. If you have a Bible verse that is challenging, type in the verse, for example, 1 John 1:9 and type John Piper behind it and you will see everything that John Piper has written on this verse.

StudyLight.org Commentaries: www.studylight.org/

> Choose from over 100 Bible Commentaries freely available online at StudyLight.org for sermon, Bible study, and Sunday school preparation.

> A biblical commentary is a written systematic series of explanations and interpretations of Scripture. They are written by some of the most knowledgeable theologians in church history. Through a personal narrative, they provide deeper understanding and insight into the Bible, and can be valuable tools to assist both casual reading and serious study.

Precept Austin: www.preceptaustin.org/

> Contains hundreds whole commentaries, verse by verse commentary collections, articles, sermons, and devotionals found through a topic list, a site

index, or question box. You will see Precept Austin come up in any search list that asks for a "commentary" query. For example, you may google, "commentary on Romans 5:"1 and a list of commentaries will come up on the screen. Almost certainly Percept Austin will be one of the options.

Bible.org/: The Lord gave the founder of Bible.org a vision for developing an internet platform so that gifted teachers could teach to millions of people by posting their good, solid Bible study material on the web. In 1994 he founded Biblical Studies Foundation (also known as Bible.org). He grew up attending a church in Texas where Hampton Keathley III was pastor for many years. It is mostly Dallas Theological Seminary professors and graduates who write the expert commentaries.

Bible gateway.com: www.biblegateway.com/

Great source for Bible verses and some commentaries.

Bible Study Tools.com: www.biblestudytools.com/ Large assortment of Bible study tools including Bible verses and commentaries.

Crosswalk.com: www.crosswalk.com/. Limited to devotional but lots of them.

Got Questions.com:www.gotquestions.org/

More than 500,000 Bible questions answered. I haven't found one they don't answer. Type your Bible related question into google and put "Got questions" behind it and most of the available answers will come up in a list.

Free-Online-Bible-Study.com: www.free-online-bible-study.com/bible-commentaries.com/

Bible Lessons International is a non-profit Bible study ministry dedicated to empowering God's people to interpret the Bible for themselves. These verse-by-verse, exegetical commentaries are committed to the trustworthiness and authority of Scripture, emphasizing the intent of the original inspired authors by means of their: Historical Setting, Literary Context, Grammatical Features, Choice of Words, Genre, and Parallel Passages.

The Blue Letter Bible: www.blueletterbible.org/.

Type any topic or verse in google and type Blue Letter Bible and hit enter. For general commentaries and other Bible study helps go to the web site and click on the Study dropdown and choose commentaries or any of a list of helps.

Christian Classics Ethereal Library: www.ccel.org/ Wide variety of Bible study sources. Look for the Home tab at the top and in the drop down choose search and then fill in the search boxes. This site is excellent but more difficult to use than the others.

Christians Unite Bible Study Aids: bible.christianunite.com.

Simple to use but limited. The resources they have are good ones.

Grace to You (John MacArthur): gty.org/

Grace to You is a teaching site that has years of Dr. MacArthur's messages mostly in print. When accessing this site just google your topic and put "John MacArthur" behind it and most of the messages will come up in a list.

Desiring God (John Piper): www.desiringgod.org/

Desiring God is a teaching site that has years of John Piper's messages mostly in print. When accessing this site just google your topic and put "John Piper" behind it and most of the messages will come up in a list.

Charles Spurgeon: www.spurgeongems.org/

Famous English preacher in the 1800's. Web site very difficult to use. When accessing this Charles Spurgeon on any biblical topic, just google your topic and put "Charles Spurgeon" behind it and most of the messages on that topic will come up in a list.

Rick Warren: pastorrick.org/

Great devotionals. You can also type in a scripture verse in google or a topic and type "Rick Warren" after it and if he has written or said anything on the topic it will come up in a list.

Charles Stanley: www.intouch.org/

Excellent source for devotionals. You can also type in a scripture verse in google or a topic and type "Charles Stanley" after it and if he has written or said anything on the topic it will come up in a list.

R. C. Sproul: www.ligonier.org/

Excellent source for devotionals. You can also type in a scripture verse in google or a topic and type "Charles Stanley" after it and if he has written or said anything on the topic it will come up in a list.

A. W. Pink: You can also type in a scripture verse in google or a topic and type "A. W. Pink" after it and if he has written or said anything on the topic it will come up in a list.

A. W. Tozer: You can also type in a scripture verse in google or a topic and type "A. W. Tozer" after it and if he has written or said anything on the topic it will come up in a list.

B. B. Warfield: www.monergism.com/

Use main site for articles he has written, or You can also type in a scripture verse in google or a topic and type "B. B. Warfield" after it and if he has written or said anything on the topic it will come up in a list.

J. I. Packer: You can also type in a scripture verse in google or a topic and type "J. I. Packer" after it and if he has written or said anything on the topic it will come up in a list.

Charles Swindoll: You can also type in a scripture verse in google or a topic and type "Charles Swindoll" after it and if he has written or said anything on the topic it will come up in a list.

John Walvoord: You can also type in a scripture verse in google or a topic and type "John Walvoord" after it and if he has written or said anything on the topic it will come up in a list.

Warren Wiersbe: You can also type in a scripture verse in google or a topic and type "Warren Wiersbe" after it and if he has written or said anything on the topic it will come up in a list.

One Place: www.oneplace.com/

You will see a list of many evangelical ministries. If you click on any go to "Articles" and there will be a list of available articles. If there is an archive tab or a devotionals tab click on it for articles and daily/weekly devotionals.

Dr. James Boice: The Bible Study Hour: https://www.oneplace.com/ministries/the-bible-study-hour/

Click on "More" then click on "Articles"

Made in the USA
Middletown, DE
08 June 2023